IMAGES

of England

HANDSWORTH

AQUEDUCT CHAIN BAR FREES
DARNALL AND HANDSWORTH BARS

Turnpike Road from Worksop in the County of Nottingham to the North East end of Attercliffe in the County of York.

A TABLE of TOLLS to be taken at this BAR pursuant to the Directions of an act passed in the sixth Year of the Reign of his Majesty King George the fourth Viz.

	s	d
For every Horse or other Beast drawing any Coach Barouche Sociable Berlin Charriot Landau Chaise Calash Gig Chair Phaeton Caravan Whiskey Hearse Litter Curricle or any Carriage on Springs drawn by more than one Horse or for any taxed Cart the sum of —		4½
For any single Horse drawing any such Coach Barouche Sociable Berlin Charriot Landau Chaise Calash Gig Chair Phaeton Caravan Whiskey Hearse Litter Curricle or any Carriage on Springs the sum of —		6
For every Horse or other Beast drawing any Waggon Wain Cart or Carriage haveing the Sole or bottom of the Fellies of the Wheels thereof of less breadth than four inches and a half the sum of —		7
For every Horse or other Beast drawing any Waggon Wain Cart or Carriage haveing the Sole or bottom of the Fellies of the Wheels thereof of the breadth of four inches and a half and under five inches and a half the sum of —		6
But if the axel tree bushes and Wheels of any such last mentioned Waggon Wain Cart or Carriage are made perfectly cylindrical the sum of —		5
For every Horse or other Beast drawing any Waggon Wain Cart or Carriage haveing the sole or bottom of the Fellies of the Wheels thereof of the breadth of five inches and a half and upwards and so as the Tire on the surface of such Wheels shall not deviate more than half an Inch from a flat and level surface and the nails of the Tire of such Wheels shall be countersunk so as not to project beyond a quarter of an inch above the surface of such Tire the sum of—		4½
But if the axel tree bushes and Wheels of any such last mentioned Waggon Wain Cart or Carriage are made perfectly cylindrical the sum of —		3½
And for every Horse or other Beast drawing any such last mentioned Waggon Wain Cart or Carriage the Wheels whereof shall not be constructed in either of the two modes last above mentioned the sum of —		6
For every Horse or other Beast drawing any Waggon Wain Cart or Carriage haveing the sole or bottom of the fellies of the Wheels thereof of a breadth not less than four and a half inches and so constructed that the Wheels run in a track the breadth of which shall be either under four feet five inches or above five feet eight inches and haveing the axel tree bushes and Wheels made perfectly cylindrical the sum of —		2½
For every Horse Mule or ass laden or unladen and not drawing the sum of —		1
For every drove of Oxen or other neat Cattle the sum of fifteen pence per score and so on in proportion for any less number —	1	5
For every drove of Calves Swine Hogs Sheep or Lambs the sum of sevenpence half penny per score and so on in proportion for any less number —		7½

ALFRED BROADHURST, CLERK to the TRUSTEES
RICHARD MARSH *Successor*

The Worksop to Attercliffe Turnpike Road ran through Handsworth. This sign from 1826 was attached to the Toll House which stood on Handsworth Road, just before the fork to Richmond Lane. The sign is now in Kelham Island Museum.

IMAGES
of England

HANDSWORTH

Compiled by
Sandra Gillott

TEMPUS

First published 1999
Copyright © Sandra Gillott, 1999

Tempus Publishing Limited
The Mill, Brimscombe Port,
Stroud, Gloucestershire, GL5 2QG

ISBN 0 7524 1633 2

Typesetting and origination by
Tempus Publishing Limited
Printed in Great Britain by
Midway Clark Printing, Wiltshire

This book is dedicated to my husband Keith, for his love, support and friendship; also to Rachel and Sarah my daughters, in the hope that Handsworth will come to mean as much to them as it does to me.

The cast of a concert party held at the Primitive Methodist chapel on Hall Road in 1923.

Contents

Acknowledgements

I would like to thank all the kind people listed below who have lent me photographs or supplied me with information to make this book possible; my grateful thanks go to them all. On a personal note I would like to thank my husband Keith for his help and patience over the last few months.

Graeme Lupton, Peter Allison, Stan Fox, Mr and Mrs Earl, Darren Coates, Mrs Broxholme, Sue Turton, Ben Clayton, Handsworth Social Club, Handsworth Historical Society, Peter King, Howard Turner, Walter Saxton, Howard Chandler, Lorraine Smith, Harold Cable, Ivan Bloodworth, Glenis Watson, Christine Hunt, Joe Muscroft.

If I have inadvertently missed anyone out I am truly sorry.

My thanks go to you all.

Introduction

Memories are like the finest champagne – when the bubbles get to the top they burst, giving great pleasure. What I am trying to do with this book is not to write a history of Handsworth, but just to evoke a few pleasant memories.

The Soke of Handsworth was once a collection of pretty villages, five miles from Sheffield town. Now it is just part of its urban sprawl. The layout of Handsworth has changed very little: its centre is still the curve on the main road, with its churches, hostelries and shops. The land, though, has altered from extensive agricultural use to large housing and industrial estates. When it was surveyed for the Domesday Book in 1086 three quarters of the Soke of Handsworth was woodland. Handsworth has always had a lot of large houses, apart from the ones on the main road, like Orgreave Hall, Rotherwood Hall, Handsworth Hall, Richmond Hall, Woodthorpe Hall, Bramley Hall and Ballifield Hall with only the latter two remaining.

This collection of photographs are mostly my own. They date back to the 1880s but now most of the older buildings have been demolished. I would like to thank all the people who have been so kind to me during the preparation of this book, lending me valuable personal photographs and giving me information. The hardest part was not what to put in but what to leave out. We the people of Handsworth are very fortunate that we have our own museum, based in the parish centre. With its own collection of old maps, photographs, school records, church records as well as artefacts of local interest.

But we should also be very grateful to all the people who have gone before us for all the work they have done especially the photographers for leaving us with the pictorial views. Also to people like Heneage Ferraby whose love of history, especially local history, has helped many people over the years, and Florence Earl who wrote her memories of Handsworth in 1896. She wrote about local people and their lives; without them I could not possibly have written this book. The book will have served its purpose if the reader gets as much pleasure from reading it as I have in compiling it.

What changes there have been in my lifetime make one wonder what changes are to come in the future, in a world which is getting progressively smaller with a pace that is quickening day by day. I just hope Handsworth can survive it.

Sandra Gillott
Chairman
Handsworth Historical Society

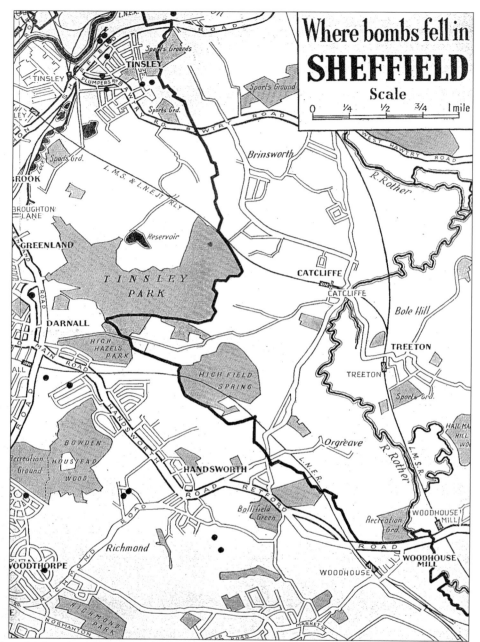

Only a few bombs were reported as falling in the Handsworth area. Two incendiary bombs were dropped on 29 August 1940 at 2.52 a.m. in the Myrtle Bank area. They were extinguished by wardens from Woodhouse EHQ Tender no. 36. Two more bombs were dropped on Athelstan Road during the night of the 15/16 December 1940. At 5 Athelstone Road damage was done to the roof, bedroom and kitchen. The fire was extinguished by auxiliary fire officer no. 1653 Taylor, by water through a stirrup pump, while on his way to report for duty. More incendiary bombs fell in the fields near the railway lines below the Finchwell area, but they burnt themselves out.

One
Darnall to the Parkway

Handsworth Hill in the 1890s. This area formed part of the old parish of Handsworth.

Trams coming up from Darnall in the 1950s.

The Knoll in 1891. This was the home of the Craven family who had a railway wagon works in Darnall.

The Knoll in 1963, when it was Sutherland's Potted Meats factory.

Looking down Handsworth Hill towards the new bridge. The houses on the left are called Melbourne Villas, Hoby House, Boston House and Eastfield and were built in 1903.

The Triangle shops in 1946 with the delivery boy's bicycle parked outside the butcher's shop.

A tram makes its way up Handsworth Hill in 1925. Trams to Handsworth ceased on 5 May 1957.

Handsworth Road at the junction of Clifton Crescent in 1957, at the time the tram tracks were taken up.

Handsworth Road in December 1957. The Octopus Café, on the left hand side, was a favourite meeting place for teenagers in the 1950s.

Clifton Square, July 1963. It is not known when these cottages were built; they probably date from the mid or late eighteenth century.

Clifton Square, July 1963, prior to their demolition. Flats now occupy this site.

Clifton House in 1907. The home of Mr and Mrs Walter Earl. To reach Clifton House one had to walk up Clifton Lane which had large trees on the right hand side up to the house and a hedge on the left, the hedge being the boundary of the nurseries belonging to Fisher, Son and Sibray.

Geoffrey Earl sitting outside Clifton House with his dog in 1907. The house is now a residential home.

The woodman's cottage at the entrance of Bowden Housteads Wood in 1890. The woodman was Mr Wilson who was succeeded by his son, Frank.

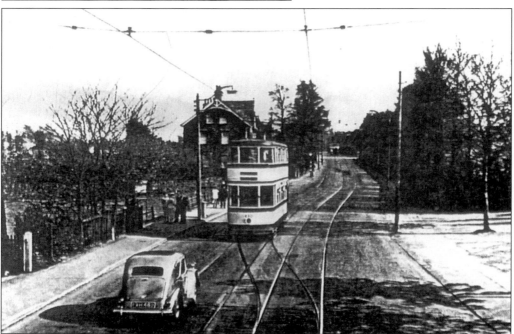

Handsworth Road. The elm trees on the right formed the boundary to Fisher, Son and Sibray nurseries. Dr O'Flynn lived in the big house in the centre of the picture which was named The Gables.

Handsworth Road in 1959, looking towards the Triangle Estate. The elm trees are now in the middle of the roundabout with Dr O'Flynn's house on the right.

A view from the fields towards Moore and Wrights, with the roundabout in the centre and the Triangle Estate on the right.

The open-air swimming pool in Bowden Housteads Wood was built in 1926 by the miners. The fence around the pool was built from railway sleepers. The water was fed to the pool by a natural spring and was very cold. In the 1990s further alterations were made to the Sheffield Parkway and the Mosborough link road was added. The swimming pool is now under the new roundabout.

Two
The Parkway to Finchwell Road

This detached house on Handsworth Road covered in dog-eared ivy was the home of
Mr B. Renshaw. Afterwards it became the home of Mr Rex L. Gray, who was a health specialist
with a gymnasium in his back garden which was sometimes used as a polling station.

Glenwood which stood on the corner of Handsworth Road and now the present Oakley Road, in 1891. Glenwood was the home of Mr Joe Sibray and Miss Sibray, and later belonged to Major and Mrs Settle. It ended its days as the Alfred Gold School of Dancing; flats now occupy the site.

This photograph, taken in 1910, is looking back down Handsworth Road with Glenwood House on the right. The next pair of houses in the centre behind the trees are both called The Poplars.

The home of Benjamin Huntsman: he lived here in 1742. It was in this cottage that he invented crucible steel. Benjamin was born in Epworth, the third son of Quaker parents. He was a clockmaker by profession, but after moving to Handsworth he started experimenting with different materials to help him with his work. The cottage was demolished in the 1930s and Benjamin is buried in the Hill Top Cemetery at Attercliffe.

Digging out to widen Handsworth Road in December 1957.

Looking back down Handsworth Road from the corner of Oakley Road. The wall on the left was the boundary of Fisher, Son and Sibrays. There was a little break in the wall, with a recess for a well named the Shilling Well.

Handsworth Road in December 1957: work is just starting on the Moore and Wright site. This building was demolished in January 1998. The Asda Hypermarket now occupies the site.

Birklands House, the home of Mr W. Atkinson, who was a Justice of the Peace as well as chairman of Fisher, Son and Sibray. Birklands House was demolished in 1948. The road to the rear of the house still retains the name.

Mr Shepherd with his son Neil in the garden outside their prefab on the Richmond Park Estate. The first prefabs were built in 1948, with 182 built in Handsworth. The authorities started to demolish them in 1969 and by 1971 all the residents had been rehoused.

A horse and cart on Handsworth Road approaching the Norfolk Hotel, *c.* 1890.

Fisher, Son and Sibray workmen standing outside the nursery gates on Handsworth Road. On the left is the glasshouse and on the right, standing in the garden, are Mr and Mrs Barks. Mr Barks was coachman to Mr Atkinson.

Looking up Park Lane (now Finchwell Road). The Norfolk Hotel is on the right.

Handsworth Quarry, c. 1900. There were three stone quarries operating in Handsworth around this time. The quarries were very deep and quite dangerous but provided work for a lot of Handsworth men. Most of the older houses in Handsworth were built with stone carved from these quarries.

Handsworth Colliery, which was at the end of Finchwell Road. The shaft was sunk in 1903. In 1968 the last pit in the Handsworth boundary closed. Coal mining had been part of Handsworth life for over 800 years.

Three
Finchwell Road to Richmond Road

Handsworth Road in December 1957.

Fisher, Son and Sibray offices on Handsworth Road. The offices were demolished in 1927 and a school now occupies the site.

Storeroom and stable for Fisher, Son and Sibray in 1891 on Handsworth Road. More recently this building was occupied by Goodyear Blackburn Ltd.

Elm House stood at the corner of Handsworth Road and Dodson Drive in 1963. The Buxton family who lived here were the owners of Handsworth Bluestone Quarry. A garage now stands on the site.

Looking up Handsworth Road, then called Main Road, in 1891.

Richmond View in 1891. It was then the home of Dr Blyth – his name can be seen over he door. It is now a dental surgery.

A general view of Main Road, Handsworth, *c.* 1890.

Handsworth post office and drapery store. Mrs Mary Allen (centre) was postmistress and on her right is Kate Bell (later Mrs Mirfin), who after Mrs Allen's death became postmistress. The house was double-fronted with the post office to the left and the drapers to the right. At Christmas time one of the upstairs rooms was turned into a toy shop. The post office had a carriage entrance at the rear.

The post office in 1965.

Oakfield House, previously the home of the Fisher family. The front of the house faced towards Richmond. The shop fronts are where the rear of the house was before. This photograph was taken in 1966.

Handsworth Road, with the Wesleyan church in the centre, *c.* 1890. All the houses on this side of the road lost their front gardens due to road widening.

Poplar Cottage on Handsworth Road, with its poplar trees in the front garden, *c*. 1890.

Poplar Cottage again, in 1964. For many years this house was lived in by the Milner family. Mr Milner was the village undertaker.

Looking back down Handsworth Road in the early 1950s, with the Wesleyan church in the centre of the picture. The grass verges are still there as the dual carriageway has not yet been built.

Manor View in 1891. The house is now a private residence. It was previously a doctor's surgery, but for many years it was the dental practice of R.K. Cole.

This red brick detached house stood on the corner of Handsworth Road and Fitzalan Road, c. 1890. Just behind the tree in the centre of the picture is a single-storey building where Mr Milner had his joinery business and Mr Tarry had his cobbler's shop.

Looking up Fitzalan Road onto Handsworth Road in 1925. The cottages on Handsworth Road have now been demolished.

Oak House at the corner of Handsworth Road and Fitzalan Road in 1891. For many years this house has been a fish and chip shop.

Leadbeater's Cottages stood where the flats on Handsworth Road are now. John Leadbeater who built the cottages lived in the end cottage and had his workshop there.

Handsworth Council School. An extract from the school's log book reads: 'This the Handsworth Infants Board School was opened for the first time on 10 February 1902. When I Edith Sarginson commenced duties with Florence Wilson as assistant.' At that time there were fifty-eight children in attendance. According to the same log book the day after opening, 11 February, the children were given a half-day holiday as it was Shrove Tuesday. The school finally closed in 1995.

Handsworth Road, *c.* 1890. The front gardens of all the cottages led to an unmade road.

Handsworth Road in 1957. The petrol station on the left belonged to Mr Norman Walker. It is now a Shell petrol station.

Main Road, Handsworth, *c.* 1890.

Laverack Street in 1926. The Laverack family lived in Handsworth Road and Mr Laverack was
held in very high esteem by the people of Handsworth, who named a road after him.

Mr Keyworth stands at the door of his butcher's shop on Handsworth Road. The shop stood near the New Crown.

The Handsworth Oak and the old village smithy at the side of the Turf Tavern. The two men on the left are Norman Walker and his father.

Pulling down the village smithy and the Handsworth Oak in 1926, to make way for Laverack Street.

1109. Handsworth. Nr. Sheffield.

Handsworth Road, c. 1910. The lady in white on the right is Mrs Sarah Ann Cutts, the village midwife.

Handsworth Road at the junction of Richmond Road. The children in the centre of the picture are standing in front of the Jeffcock Memorial Fountain. William Jeffcock of High Hazels was the first Mayor of Sheffield in 1843. The second Mayor of Sheffield was his cousin, Thomas Dunn of Richmond Hill.

Handsworth Road at the junction of Richmond Road. The New Crown is in the centre of the picture.

The service to commemorate the re-siting of the Jeffcock Memorial Fountain on 8 July 1988. The fountain had been damaged in a car accident the previous year. Members of the Handsworth Historical Society look on.

The Plaza Cinema, designed by local architect Bernard Powell of Woodhouse. The cinema opened on 27 December 1937. *The Plainsman*, starring Gary Cooper and Jean Arthur, was the first film shown. It closed as a cinema on 29 September 1963 and re-opened as a bingo hall the following week. It then became a snooker hall and now houses both snooker and ten-pin bowling.

The Brightside and Carbrook Co-operative Society at the corner of Hendon Street and Hall Road. Prior to 1921 Hendon Street was called Henry Street, the road name was altered when Handsworth was incorporated into the City of Sheffield.

Three stone cottages on Hendon Street in 1908. Only two of them have names, Aviary Cottage and Braden Stoke Cottage.

Four

The Bramley Estate

Myrtle Bank Farm which has now been demolished. It was originally part of the Bramley Hall Estate. For many years this land was farmed by the Mottram family.

Myrtle Bank Farm stood behind St Mary's church and to the left of the Bramley Estate and stretched over to Woodhouse. The farm buildings were demolished by Sheffield Council in 1980; only its foundations and a few stone gate pillars remain.

Hay-making at Myrtle Bank Farm.

Bramley Hall, *c.* 1910. The first mention of Bramley was in 1205, when it was given to the Monks of Kirkstead by Henry, son of Robert De Lovetot.

Bramley Hall after 1922 when the extension had been added. The hall is steeped in history and is believed to be one of the few residences in Sheffield to retain a ha-ha. The building to the left belonged to Sadlers, the coal merchant.

Annie and Ernest Oliver (left) and Elsie and Herbert Oliver (right), who lived in Bramley Hall from 1922 to 1972. The two brothers extended the house and divided it in two.

The magnificent fireplace in the drawing room is mid-Victorian, made from polished oak and carved in an outstanding design with tiled insets.

The Firth Window in the Hall is outstanding with glass-leaded windows and two Tuscan pillars. The crest on the window reads *Deo non Fortuna*, (God, not Fortune), but it is not known to which family the crest belonged.

These two footprints are etched into the flashing of the roof in Bramley Hall. The one on the left is marked EBK 1895. The square-toed shoe on the right is dated 1850. There are three other prints with various dates etched on them on the roof.

Tommy Bond's dairy at the top of Bramley Lane in 1920. The Plaza Cinema was built on this site on which originally stood the lodge to Bramley Hall. Just before the Second World War Bond's moved across the road to their present site.

Bramley Lane in 1928, looking up towards Handsworth Road.

Looking down Bramley Lane in 1930. Mr Tommy Staniforth is standing in the lane to the right, with the allotments on the left.

The first houses being built on the Bramley Estate in 1935. The estate was built by Ernest and Herbert Oliver of Bramley Hall. The first pair of houses to be built were no. 1 Bramley Avenue and no. 28 Bramley Park Road.

Singing for the Whitsuntide parade in front of the Bramley shops in 1947.

An advertisement for Sansam Bros
Ltd.

Five
Hendon Street to St Joseph's Road

Handsworth Road at the junction of Richmond Road. St Mary's church is in the centre of the picture, with the signpost on the right showing the way to Richmond and Intake.

Handsworth Road at the junction of Richmond Road (previously Britton Hill) and Henry Street (now Hendon Street).

Handsworth Road, *c.* 1900.

Numbers 351-357 Handsworth Road in 1960.

Mrs Elizabeth Stacey with her granddaughter Kathleen Cardwell outside the home of Mrs Stacey, no. 357 Handsworth Road.

Numbers 361-369 Handsworth Road in 1960.

Handsworth Road in 1951. The butcher's shop belonged to Mr L.C. Gray. Mrs Peggy Hughes is in the centre of the picture with her dog.

Numbers 371-377 Handsworth Road in 1960. All the cottages on Handsworth Road were demolished in 1963 to make way for flats.

Numbers 379-393 Handsworth Road in 1960.

The same cottages in around 1950, before the fronts were rendered.

These flats now occupy all the land where the stone cottages stood.

OLIVERS

THE BUTCHERS, HANDSWORTH

(NEAR FOUNTAIN)

HIGHEST QUALITY MEAT

AT

LOWEST PRICES.

An advertisement for Olivers butchers.

Handsworth Road, *c.* 1970.

An advertisement for the Bon Bon shop.

St Mary's church parade on Handsworth Road in 1953.

An advertisement for Hughes' drinks shop.

HUGHES

THE ORIGINAL DRINK SHOP

for

HOT AND COLD DRINKS.

❖

Sweets,

Tobacco, Cigarettes.

❖

A GOOD ASSORTMENT OF
Herbs, etc.   **Patent Medicines.**

❖

364, HANDSWORTH ROAD,

HANDSWORTH.

St Mary's church parade on Handsworth Road in 1953. The small building in the middle belonged to Handsworth Motor Company and to the right of that stood Boots Cash Chemist.

An advertisement for The Handsworth Motor Company.

Looking back along Handsworth Road in 1966. The Plaza Cinema is on the right.

Handsworth Road, *c.* 1915. The building on the left is still a newsagent's and the building with the extension to the front is now a bookmaker's.

Handsworth Road with a tram passing St Mary's church, *c.* 1950.

Brightside & Carbrook Co-operative Society Ltd, Handsworth Road, in 1903.

The newsagent's on Handsworth Road in 1917 which belonged to the Sprigg family.

Handsworth Road showing the rectory gardener's cottage, which was pulled down by order of Sheffield Corporation under the provisions of the 1931 Slum Clearance Act. Lidster, the monumental mason, occupied the site which now houses a car salesroom.

An aerial photograph of Handsworth Road in 1960.

Handsworth Endowed School on the left with the Endowed School Rooms on the right, at the corner of St Joseph's Road and Handsworth Road.

Handsworth Endowed School on St Joseph's Road. The building is now occupied by a tyre company.

Six

The Road to Woodhouse

Children outside St Mary's church. The Cross Keys public house is on the right with a pair of dray horses coming up the road.

Underwood's motor bus travels down Handsworth Road past the Old Crown public house in 1934. The road was quite narrow at this time.

Horses coming up Handsworth Road past the Old Crown Public House on the right. Clough Road, now Medlock Road, is on the left. Jubbs cottages, now demolished, are on the right.

Miners walking up Handsworth Road. There are no bungalows as yet on the left and the road still looks like a country lane.

The bungalows on the left-hand side of Handsworth Road. The large house at the bottom was East Bank.

Cliffe Hill on Handsworth Road was for a long time the home of the Jubb family. Afterwards it became Dr Nelson's surgery and now it is a nursing home.

Miners walking up Handsworth Road past Cliffe Hill. The ornate archway over the gate was removed in the late 1980s.

Kent House on Handsworth Road. The house in the centre behind the trees is now Handsworth Working Men's Club.

The rear of Handsworth Working Men's Club in 1967. The house was originally the home of Mr Littlewood, who was the founder of what was Fisher, Son and Sibray.

The beginning of the process to widen Handsworth Road before the construction of the bungalows.

Claremont and Belmont: two of the Victorian villas on Handsworth Road just after the junction of Handsworth Grange Road.

Looking up Handsworth Road in December 1957.

East Bank House stands at the top of Orgreave Lane where it joins Handsworth Road. The Atkinson family and the Buxton family were among its occupants. It was demolished in December 1967. Sheffield Corporation Tramways no. 501 is pictured in May 1952.

The junction of Orgreave Lane and what was previously named Worksop Road, now Retford Road. The village pinfold was on Orgreave Lane.

This was the site of the tram terminus in 1957. The trams used to run only as far as the Norfolk Hotel, but in 1934 the line was extended to here. East Bank House is on the right.

Looking down Retford Road, c. 1950. These houses overlook Ballifield Hall.

Looking up Retford Road, towards the tram terminus, c. 1950.

Ballifield Hall in 1925. The Stacey family lived at Ballifield Hall for many years: in 1378 it was recorded that John Stacye of Ballifield was taxed four times as much as the majority. In 1666 because of religious persecution Malon Stacey, his wife, children and several servants left England for a new life in Trents Town (which was later shortened to Trenton), USA. There they founded a Quaker colony and Malon built a himself a home and a grist mill. He owned 3,500 acres of land which he called Ballifield. His residence was called Dore House. Ballifield Hall was also lived in by the Jubb and Cadman families, but for many years now it has been a children's home.

Dore House Lodge on Retford Road. The Bonnington family lived here. Mr Bill Bonnington worked for Joseph Helliwell at Dore House Farm which was to the rear.

Looking up Retford Road with Dore House Lodge on the right-hand side. Ballifield Hall stands on the left.

The junction of Retford Road and Beaverhill Road in 1925. The Dore House Industrial Estate now occupies land to the left of the picture.

Rotherham Road was re-aligned from the eastern side of Dore House farm to the western side when these houses were built.

Helliwell's farm on Rotherham Road in July 1963. The land was later used to build an Asda store, but the wall has always been retained.

Looking over Highfield Lane with Orgreave Coke Ovens at the rear, in 1990.

Orgreave Coke Oven. The oven was built in 1918 and demolished in 1990.

Part of the Grange Estate which was owned by Fisher, Son and Sibray Ltd. The Atkinson and Wake families lived in the house in later years, until the whole estate was sold for housing development in 1963. The Beaver Estate was built on the site. This building was the office block.

Grange Lodge in 1891, part of the Cinderhill Estate. The Wake family lived in the house at this time.

The Grange coach house in 1963. The coach house stood at the end of Grange Lane, near to the Quaker burial grounds.

Grange House gates in 1920, looking towards the house.

The end of Grange Lane, *c.* 1940. Grange Lane starts on the Bramley Estate and finishes in what is now Beaver Hill Road.

Bank House, *c.* 1930. George Fox, founder of the Society of Friends, is said to have hidden in the cellars of this house in 1666, after speaking at Cinderhill Green. The lady in the picture is Mrs Harding and the boy is Maurice Henry Little.

The Quaker burial ground, Cinderhill, in 1951. Most of the Stacey family of Ballifield Hall are buried here.

Beaver Hill Road, c. 1930. On the left is the end of Grange Lane.

Seven

The Road to Richmond

Briton Hill, *c.* 1900. The name was later changed to Richmond Lane then finally to Richmond Road. These cottages were demolished in the 1970s and flats now occupy the site.

Members of the Sanderson family outside their home on Richmond Road in 1895.

The same cottages in 1891. The street is just a country lane from Richmond, and Laverack Street has not yet been built.

A general view of Handsworth from Sanderson's fields, *c*. 1935 . The fields are now occupied by the Haigh Moor Estate.

The rear of no. 130 Richmond Road. The horses had won first prize in the Handsworth and District Carnival in 1916.

Richmond Road, *c.* 1930. Gas lamps were installed along this road in 1883.

Moulton Villas on Richmond Road in 1940. These houses were built in 1914.

Mrs Wigley outside the nursery store in 1964. The shop is now demolished, a small housing estate now occupies this site.

Richmond Road, 1936. Property on both sides of the road was demolished to make way for the development of the Mosborough Link Road, which now runs underneath this part of Richmond Road.

Sea Breeze Terrace (named after a racehorse), in 1967. Turner's shop was used by all the pupils going to Brook School.

The east front of Richmond Park, with sheep grazing. The low roofed building dates from around 1720 and Bernard Young added the taller building, which faces south, in 1885. The large number of bedrooms and attics were required because the family had ten children and a large staff. There was also a Catholic chapel attached. Richmond Lane was re-routed away from the front of the house in 1882.

A car leaving Richmond Park in 1925.

1080 Ivy Cottage, Richmond, Nr. Handsworth.

Ivy Cottage on Richmond Lane, later Richmond Road, *c.* 1910.

Richmond post office in 1890.

A second house known as Ivy Cottage on Richmond Road, c. 1910. This one stood directly across the road from the other Ivy Cottage.

Richmond Old Hall Farm in 1963. Burrows Trippett rebuilt the farm in 1692. The Duke of Norfolk insisted on the closing of Sheffield Park gates, so carts were compelled to reach Sheffield via Gleadless or Darnall. Burrows Trippett led the opposition. The gate posts were probably removed to Trippett's farm in Richmond Road where they still remain.

Richmond College, c. 1980. The college officially opened on 20 October 1966 and closed in July 1997. It changed its name from Richmond College to Stradbroke College and finally became part of the Sheffield College.

Woodthorpe Hall, c. 1890. The Parker family came to live here in the middle of the eighteenth century and remained until John Parker was made Deputy Lord Lieutenant of the West Riding of Yorkshire; for sixty years he was a magistrate in Sheffield. The Parkers were primarily bankers. John was elected the first Member of Parliament for Sheffield in 1832. He was later Secretary to the Admiralty and a Privy Councillor and was created Lord Darrington.

Woodthorpe Hall, c. 1900. In 1845 Woodthorpe Hall was occupied by John Bower Brown and his family, who remained there until 1876. They were followed by the Gainsford family. The front of the house was covered in ivy. Each room was painted a different colour. It was demolished in 1934 to make way for the Woodthorpe Estate and school. The house stood where the swimming baths used to be.

Eight

The Churches

One of the earliest drawings of St Mary's church, by Rowland Hibbard in 1824. Rowland Hibbard was one of the most famous watercolour artists of his time. He was churchwarden of St Mary's in 1820 and lived a somewhat uneventful life as a gentleman at Lamb Hill, Richmond.

Looking towards St Mary's church from St Joseph's Road, *c.* 1910. St Mary's church was founded around 1170 by the De Lovetot family. The house on the left covered in dog-eared ivy was occupied by Mr Scott, the village saddler.

St Mary's church from St Joseph's Road, fifty years later. The church spire was destroyed by lightning in 1698 and the steeple was rebuilt, but it was so small and squat it was nicknamed Handsworth Stump. The last time the spire was struck by lightning was 1978.

Lidster & Son Ltd Monumental Masons, outside St Mary's church in 1971.

-1914- -1918-

THE PEAL OF EIGHT BELLS & CLOCK, WERE PLACED IN THE TOWER OF St MARY'S CHURCH, HANDSWORTH, BY
PARISHIONERS, & FRIENDS, TO THE GLORY OF GOD, & IN LASTING MEMORY OF THESE MEN OF HANDSWORTH,
& RICHMOND, WHO GAVE THEIR LIVES, FOR THEIR COUNTRY, IN THE GREAT WAR.

ASPLAND, ERIC.	DOWD, JAMES.	MARCHANT, SIDNEY.
ATKIN, ROBERT.	EASTWOOD, ALLAN.	MASON, RICHARD.
BALL, GERALD WHEATLEY.	ELLIS, HUBERT VICTOR.	METCALFE, CHARLES FREDᵏ.
BARSBY, CLARENCE.	ETTWELL, WILLIAM HEDLEY.	NORTH, SLEAFORD THOMAS.
BILLARD, JAMES.	ETTWELL, FRANK.	RUTTER, JOSEPH.
BILTON, SAMUEL C.	FAULKNER, FRANK ELLIOTT.	SAXTON, LEONARD OSBORN.
BISHOP, JACOB.	FLETCHER, ARTHUR.	SHARP, THOMAS.
BROWNETT, THOMAS WARD.	GARTH, HERBERT.	SHAW, HIRAM.
BRUNT, EDGAR.	GODDARD, ARTHUR.	SHERWIN, SIDNEY.
BULMER, WILLIAM HENRY.	GRATTON, FRANK.	SKEELS, HERBERT DAVENPORT D.C.M
BUXTON, PERCY GEORGE.	HALL, OSWALD.	SPENCER, HARRY.
CAWTHORNE, JOHN THOMAS.	HOLLAND, DONALD FRAZER.	SWINDALL, GEORGE.
CLOUGH, CLARENCE SCHOFIELD.	HUTCHINSON, JOHN HENRY.	TUXFORD, WILLIAM.
COOKE, CHARLES GEORGE.	KENT, ERNEST.	WARHURST, GEORGE ARTHUR.
COX, ELI.	LAKIN, ERNEST.	WHITE, SAM.
CUTTS, GEORGE.	LAXTON, JOSEPH WALTER.	WIGGINS GEORGE.
DOWD, PATRICK.	LIDGETT, WILLIAM.	WADE, GEORGE.

"LEST WE FORGET."   DECEMBER 1920.

The war memorial to the men of Handsworth and Richmond who gave their lives for their country. This stands on Handsworth Road outside St Mary's church.

The bell in the centre is the Shrewsbury Bell given in 1590 by George Talbot, 6th Earl of Shrewsbury. The outer pair by T. Mears have since been melted down. This photograph was taken in 1919 when a new peal of eight bells and a new clock were installed as a war memorial.

St Mary's church was the first in the city to get a stainless steel roof. Only four other churches in the United Kingdom have one.

The notice board in St Mary's church grounds in 1964.

No.1111. Handsworth. Nr. Sheffield.

The Wesleyan church on Handsworth Road in 1891.

The Wesleyan church on Handsworth Road, c. 1900.

In memory of the men of the Handsworth Wesleyan Cricket Club who died in the First World War.

The Wesleyan church on Handsworth Road, *c.* 1920.

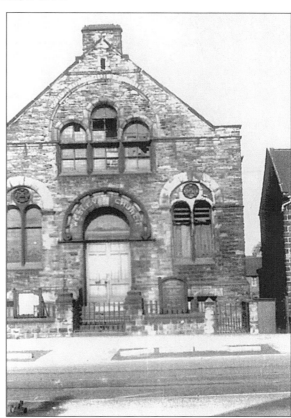

The Wesleyan church after it was gutted by fire in January 1956. The church was reopened again in 1960.

Mrs Shaw outside Holly Lodge, which is now the Christian Life Centre on Handsworth Road.

Richmond Wesleyan Reform Chapel, founded in 1852.

The Primitive Methodist chapel on Hall Road, which was demolished to make way for a library. This in turn has also been demolished. Four houses now stand on this land.

An earlier photograph of the Primitive Methodist chapel.

St Joseph's church was solemnly opened on 7 June 1881. The money to build the church, school and Presbytery was donated by the Duke of Norfolk.

The interior of St Joseph's church, showing seven of the beautifully carved Stations of the Cross, which were donated by the family of Adrian Van Roosmalen.

Nine
Public Houses

The Norfolk Hotel, Handsworth Road, in 1904. The landlord, George Wilby, is second from the left. The first reference to the Norfolk Hotel was in 1841 when Mr Green was the landlord.

The Norfolk Hotel, Handsworth Road. Mrs Abdy is the lady cleaning windows. This was originally the tram terminus for Handsworth.

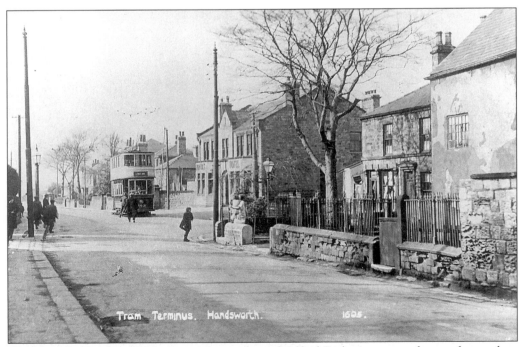

Tram Terminus. Handsworth. 1605.

The Norfolk Hotel, c. 1920. Across the road stood Alfred Barber's grocery shop and next door was Mr Crawshaw the butcher.

Orgreave miners outside the Cross Keys. the Cross Keys was originally the church house, then a school. In 1800 it was sold by the churchwardens to the parish clerk, Joseph Smith for £43. In 1804 it was granted an ale licence.

The Cross Keys in 1891. The first building on this site is thought to have dated back to 1250.

The rear of the Cross Keys. This is one of the few public houses to be situated in church grounds and the only one to have graves in the back garden!

The Cross Keys, *c.* 1940. This view clearly shows the three extensions to the old church house. The original building is in the centre with a later extension to the right, then a porch and finally the living quarters.

The Old Crown next door to the Cross Keys on Handsworth Road.

Looking up Handsworth Road towards the Old Crown, *c.* 1924. Jubbs Cottages are on the left and Clough Road (now Medlock Road) is off to the right.

The Cross Keys and the Old Crown, with the churchyard in between, *c.* 1970.

The Turf Tavern. The first reference to a beerhouse on this site was in 1833; it was originally attached to the old village smithy.

Mr John Henry Wilson with his staff and customers outside the New Crown Inn, *c.* 1891.

Mr John Henry Wilson outside the New Crown Inn. The first reference to this establishment as a beer house was in 1833.

Handsworth Social Club on Hall Road, *c.* 1970. This building was originally the new Reading Rooms (the old Reading Rooms were on the main road). It was built privately, for the sole use of the villagers, with money donated by the Scott family. The stone used was from the family's quarry and the men who dressed the stone did the work for free.

Ten
The Parish Centre

Church Lane in the 1920s. it has hardly altered at all in the last seventy years. There used to be a gate at the top of the lane and also at the side stood a wicket gate for the public footpath to Woodhouse, but this was removed when the war memorial was erected.

Looking underneath the dovecotes towards the rectory gardens in 1920. The first mention of the dovecote was in 1535. The archway had double doors at each end and doors on both sides to the stables and the coach house.

The rectory and kitchen gardens in 1920. The kitchen gardens were self-sufficient, there was even a warm wall for growing peaches. The rectory gardener had his own cottage at the top of Church Lane but this was demolished in 1931.

The Maypole dancers outside the rectory, *c.* 1903. The pole had three cockerels on the top. In 1950 the pole was lent out but never returned.

CHURCH & RECTORY. HANDSWORTH. No3

The church and the rectory. The greenhouse was removed along with the stables, hen house, wash house, brew house, coal house and other outbuildings in 1959. The present hall was opened in 1962.

The holly hedge on the south side of the rectory, showing many varieties of the famous Handsworth holly.

Looking over the rectory kitchen gardens to Jubbs Cottages which are undergoing demolition, c. 1955.

The original dovecotes before restoration. In 1535 it was recorded that the house, gardens, dovecotes and land were worth 31s 2d.

The wattle and daub wall hidden within the structure of the centre of the present building, dating from the sixteenth century. During alterations in 1959 this was plastered over.

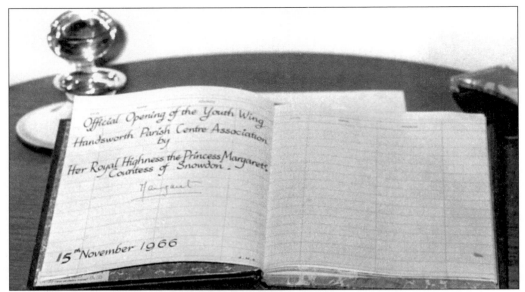

Princess Margaret's signature after the official opening of the Youth Wing on 15 November 1966.

The Youth Wing after the official opening. It was built to accommodate young people between the ages of fourteen and twenty. It was open five nights a week with its own coffee bar, kitchen, a hall downstairs for dancing, table tennis etc., and upstairs two further rooms, one fully equipped with sewing machines, the other with wood-working benches and lathes.

Eleven

The People

Mr 'Daddy' Rooke, schoolmaster, and Mrs Rooke, schoolmistress, with the children in 1895 outside the Endowed School.

Handsworth Rovers, *c.* 1914. Handsworth Rovers were formed in 1893 in the kitchen of a house in Bernard Road, now Hall Road.

Handsworth District Carnival, 1916.

Handsworth Church Football Club in the 1932-33 season, with the cup and shield. Revd Baker is at the extreme right.

Handsworth Ladies' Cricket Team, 1928. They played on the recreation ground. The lady at the front on the left was Esther Butcher, who opened the batting and was also the fast bowler.

Soldiers and the Church Boys' Brigade with Revd Baker in the Glebe Fields, 1917.

Father Adrian Van Roosmalen was appointed parish priest of St Joseph's in 1875. He served the parish for nearly fifty years and is buried in St Joseph's cemetery. He was buried on the feast of St Joseph, 19 March 1924. He was held in very high esteem by all the villagers of Handsworth.

Revd William Baker with his wife Hilda and
son Francis. He was rector from 1915 to 1943.

Heneage Ferraby with Princess Margaret at the opening of the Youth Wing on 15 November
1966. Heneage Ferraby was rector from 1944 to 1981.

Members of Handsworth Girl Guides at camp at Barnston near Bridlington in 1937.

KS TO GOD"

"FORWARD WITH RESOLUTION

The Festival of Britain parade outside the Endowed School rooms in 1951. The children on the float were all dressed as nursery rhyme characters.

The Coronation pageant of 1953. The children dressed up in costumes from all the different Commonwealth countries.

St Mary's church fête, opened by Max Bygraves, in 1950. Pictured from left to right are: Margaret Bradford as Miss Ireland, Mary Lilley as Miss Scotland, Margaret Wilkinson as Miss England, Wendy Danial as Miss Wales.

The Handsworth Sword Dancers, 1909 and 1910 team, outside the New Crown Inn.

The Handsworth Sword Dancers dancing outside St Mary's church as they still do every Boxing Day.

Girls from Brook School receive their Bronze Duke of Edinburgh's Award at Sheffield Town Hall in 1960. Back row: the Lady Mayoress, -?-, Brenda Young, -?-, -?-, Pat Rigden, -?-, Janet Marcroft. Front row: Sandra Cooper, Mary Donson, -?-, the Lord Mayor, Mary Hogg, -?-, Eileen Lee.

Mr Percy Walker, a greengrocer, with his horse and cart. His son and daughter are sitting on the cart outside St Mary's church. Mr Walker was Town Crier for many years.

The 273 Handsworth Scouts in 1957. The photograph was taken inside the Endowed School rooms by Mr Jack Holmes, a local photographer who lived on Fitzalan Road.

The May Queen and her retinue from Handsworth CUC in 1907.